Evaluating Internet Web Sites:

An Educator's Guide

KATHLEEN SCHROCK

About the Author

Kathleen Schrock is currently the Technology Coordinator for the Dennis-Yarmouth Regional School District on Cape Cod, Massachusetts. She works daily with the teachers in the district to find the best ways to incorporate technology into the curriculum at all levels and in all subject areas. She is an adjunct faculty member at Bridgewater State College and a regular contributor to *Technology Connection, Multimedia Schools*, and The MASTER Teacher's *Technology Pathfinder for Teachers* and *Technology Pathfinder for Administrators*.

Kathy is the creator of "Kathy Schrock's Guide for Educators" (http://www.capecod.net/schrockguide/), a classified, annotated site of over 1200 links to help educators enhance the curriculum and expand their professional growth. Since its inception in June of 1995, this site and its creator have received numerous awards, including a 1996 Technology Pathfinder Award from MassCUE (the Massachusetts affiliate of ISTE), a spot on Electronic Learning's "Top Ten Sites for Educators," the invitation to consult on a Web site design for Annenberg/CPB (Corporation for Public Broadcasting), and the recent election as one of National Education and Technology Alliance/Classroom Connects STARS, a group of distinguished educators and students who are bringing the Internet to life in local schools.

© Copyright 1997 by The MASTER Teacher, Inc.

All rights reserved. No part of this book may be reproduced or transmitted in any form or by any means, electronic or mechanical, including photocopying, recording, or by any information storage and retrieval system, without permission in writing from the publisher, with this exception: the Web Site Rating Form (page 3) the Evaluation Surveys for Students (pages 10-14) and the transparencies (pages 22-29) may be reproduced by school teachers or administrators for instructional use only, not for resale.

The MASTER Teacher, Inc.
Publisher
Leadership Lane
Manhattan, Kansas 66502-0038

ISBN 0-914607-48-0
Printed in the United States of America

Introduction

Critiquing information on the Internet is just an old way of looking at a new medium. Guidelines for evaluating information in print sources have existed for years. Looking at the author's credentials, the date of publication, the list of sources, and the name of the publisher gives the reader some clues as to the validity of the document. Because it is so easy to publish on the Internet (on the World Wide Web in particular), the amount of information available is growing rapidly. The material may not be edited or sponsored by an organization you are familiar with, or even provide information about the author.

As the Internet begins to carry more and more primary- and secondary-source material, administrators, teachers, and students may begin to use it frequently to supplement the curriculum. **Learning how to use the Internet is not difficult; learning to separate the quality information from the mis- and disinformation is the hard part.**

This booklet provides educators with the tools needed to learn how to effectively evaluate a Web site.

Once you feel comfortable with this evaluation process, it will become second nature to teach these same methods to your students to educate them about information validity on the Internet.

How this guide is organized

☞ **The First Step:** preparing to think critically about the Web.

☞ **Web Site Rating Form:** a checklist for teachers to use in evaluating Web sites.

☞ **Explanation of Questions from Web Site Rating Form:** a detailed explanation of each of the questions in the Web Site Rating Form. As you become familiar with this section and understand the reasons behind the questions, it will become much easier to instruct students in the evaluation process. The questions consider Web sites from four aspects:
- Technical and Design Features
- Navigation
- Authorship and Authority
- Content

☞ **Evaluation Surveys for Students:** a set of Web site evaluation sheets for students at the elementary, middle, and secondary grade levels. The student worksheets contain some higher order, critical thinking questions that require students to use the information from the checklist portion to justify use of a certain Web page.

☞ **Lesson Plan and Transparencies:** instructions for teaching how to evaluate Web sites.

☞ **Glossary of Terms:** definitions of the technology terms used in this guide.

☞ **References:** suggested resources for additional reading.

The First Step

Almost any topic, no matter how obscure, has a Web page devoted to it. There are Web pages on everything from classic cereal boxes to tours of government buildings and everything in between. To publish a page on the Internet, all the author needs is some disk space on a computer that is always hooked to the Internet (called a server). Once the information is loaded up to this server, anyone with a connection to the Internet can access it.

Unlike the print publishing world, there is little or no editorial review of material on the Internet. No official agency or subject matter specialist reviews the information before it becomes available for all to see. This presents a challenging problem for teachers and students. They have a massive amount of information at their fingertips, but is it worthwhile? Is it factual? Is the Internet really the best place to go to obtain the information?

Ferdi Serim and Melissa Koch, in their book *NetLearning: Why Teachers Use the Internet*, present a list of circumstances under which the use of the Internet in the classroom would be particularly recommended—that is, when the information being sought is:
- not in your classroom textbooks or library;
- based on data collected by governments or public interest groups;
- likely to require specialized knowledge;
- best understood from eyewitness accounts; or
- fast-breaking news (voting results, earthquakes, economic data).[1]

When it has been decided that the Internet is the best place to go to get the information, students must realize that they need a set of criteria to evaluate Internet information. If they don't do anything else, students have to verify information from the Web in a second source, preferably a print source. However, there are also many other elements of a Web page that should be considered when evaluating it for use in a project. Some of these considerations are technical, some are navigational, and the most important ones are content-related. The Web Site Rating Form on the following page provides a concise, systematic approach to considering all these elements. Each point is then discussed at length on the pages following the Rating Form.

Note: Depending on students' experience level, it may be most productive for the teacher to complete this form and then have students complete one of the surveys on pages 10-14.

Web Site Rating Form

URL: _____

SITE NAME: _____

Technical and Design Features	YES	NO	N/A
1. Does the Web page extend beyond the side edges of the monitor?			
2. Does the Web page require extensive downward scrolling to read the information?			
3. Are there useful headings and subheadings on the page?			
4. Does the page contain graphics?			
• If so, do they support the information presented on the site?			
• If so, are they appropriately sized for loading at 14.400 kbps or better?			
5. When graphics are turned off, are there text alternatives?			
6. Are the grammar and spelling on the page correct?			
7. Do icons clearly represent what is intended?			
8. Is the type large enough for use by someone who is vision-impaired?			
9. Can the site be used via a text-based browser?			
10. Does the site adhere to conventional HTML 2.0/3.0 rules?			
11. Is multimedia appropriately incorporated?			
12. Can the site be accessed reliably at any time of day?			
Navigation			
13. If an image map is present, are there also text alternatives?			
14. Are there links back to the home page from the supporting pages?			
15. Are name references used wisely to move you to another part of the same Web page?			
16. Do external and internal links work?			
17. Is the overall site "user-friendly"?			
18. Is a search tool available for the site's content?			
19. Is the resource organized logically for its intended audience/purpose? (i.e. hierarchical, branching, etc.)			
Authorship and Authority			
20. Is the page signed with a name and an e-mail address?			
21. Is information about the author given?			
22. Is the author affiliated with a recognized institution?			
23. Does the author's affiliation appear to bias the information?			
Content			
24. Is the purpose/mission of the site stated?			
25. Is the date of last update included?			
26. Has the site been revised recently?			
27. Is the information on the site factual in nature?			
28. Does the information appear to be opinion rather than fact?			
29. Does the site contain original information?			
30. Is a bibliography included of the sources/sites consulted?			
31. Does the information appear accurate? (Is it verifiable in a traditional print source?)			
32. Does the site fulfill the stated purpose?			
33a. Does the site contain primary-source material?			
33b. If the site reports research, are research methodologies and results given?			
33c. If the site contains writings, are the entire documents included?			
34. Does the site include links to relevant outside sites?			
35. Is there a form or method of offering comments about the site included?			
36. Does the content seem to add to the existing body of knowledge about the topic?			

© 1966 Kathleen Schrock (kschrock@capecod.net)

Explanation of Questions from Web Site Rating Form

Following, you will find a discussion of each of the questions on the Web Site Rating Form, which will be useful for you when you begin to evaluate pages. Elements of effective Web site design are included in the discussion of the evaluation criteria, so these questions will also be helpful if you are thinking of creating your own Web site.

Technical and Design Features

1. Does the Web page extend beyond the sides of the monitor?
It is quite disconcerting to have to scroll sideways as well as up and down to see all of the information on a Web page. Imagine if these words continued past the edge of the page, wrapped around to the next, and then continued on another line, back on this page! It is customary for some browsers, such as Netscape Navigator for the Macintosh, to open up smaller than the full screen. It is easier to use a Web page no wider than about 470 pixels, since Web pages of this width do not usually require sideways scrolling.

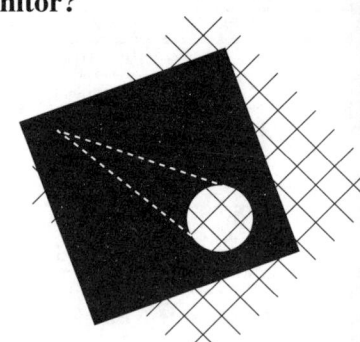

2. Does the Web page require too much downward scrolling to read the information?
The vertical viewable area of a browser is quite small, and most Web pages will naturally require the user to scroll downward to access all the information on the page. However, if a page seems to go on and on forever, perhaps it is not well-designed. The author probably should have broken up the information into logical segments and created separate Web pages with hypertext links to connect them.

3. Are there useful headings and subheadings on the page?
The original Hypertext Markup Language (HTML) conventions included designations of heading sizes one through six which would allow the Web page designer to differentiate between levels of importance of the information. Well-designed Web pages should include headings and subheadings that explain the content, as well as demonstrate the relative levels of the information. Think of the headings as items in a traditional outline format where the designations (I., A., 1., a.) indicate where the information resides in the hierarchy.

4. Does the page contain graphics?
One of the best aspects of the Web is graphical display; on the other hand, this can also be one of the worst! Graphics should be useful and appropriately sized; the rule of thumb is that they should be no larger than 35K. If a graphic needs to be larger than this, the Web page designer should offer a smaller version (called a thumbnail) that allows users to select the larger graphic if they wish to wait for the longer loading time. Large corporate headings are not a sign of a well-designed Web page. Webmasters should remember that many users are still utilizing 14.4 kbps modems to access the Net, and the wait time for a large graphic to load is significantly longer on a slower modem.

5. When graphics are turned off, are there text alternatives?
Not everyone has graphical access to the Web, a fast modem, or unlimited online time.

Some users are still accessing the Net via text-based systems (such as Lynx) and slow modems. The text-based browsers only show the designation "[IMAGE]" on their screen as a placeholder for a graphic image. Graphical browsers have a feature that allows the user to turn off the graphics to quicken the download time of the Web page. A well-designed Web page includes a text alternative that succinctly describes the image for Lynx users and those who have their graphics turned off.

6. Are the grammar and spelling on the page correct?
There is nothing more indicative of a Webmaster who is in a hurry and/or doesn't care about the quality of his or her pages than spelling and grammatical errors. No matter how useful the content is, it is hard to justify using a Web site with these all-too-common problems. However, if you or your students see a stray spelling or grammatical error on a page, let the Webmaster know. It may have just missed the spell checker.

There is one exception that should be taken into consideration. If English is the second language of the Webmaster, you may be a bit more lenient in accepting spelling and grammatical errors.

7. Do icons clearly represent what is intended?
If the page uses navigational icons, such as arrows, mailboxes, and speaker icons, they should be small in size and resolution, easy to read, and understandable to even neophyte Internet users. The navigation should also correctly lead you to an identifiable part of the site and not leave you stranded somewhere.

8. Is the type large enough for use by someone who is visually impaired?
There are entire Web sites devoted to the design of pages for those who are visually impaired. Suffice it to say that the default size browser type (12pt Times New Roman) should be the minimum for a Web page. Some browsers even allow the user to increase the type size for his or her local machine. Most of the formatting of Web pages is destroyed when this is done, but since content is foremost, it is a reasonable tradeoff.

9. Can the site be used via a text-based browser?
Viewing of graphics via a text-based browser has already been discussed. Another issue involves accessing a page that includes the new features of Web page design and HTML, especially tables and frames. Text-based browsers will not support tables, and the result on the screen is a few lines of very condensed, out-of-order text. A well-designed Web site allows an option to use a page that is "text-only" and provides the same information as the table page. Frames are not supported at all by text-based browsers, so a good Web page will also allow alternatives for those using these browsers, as well as earlier versions of the graphical browsers.

10. Does the site adhere to conventional HTML 2.0/3.0+ rules?
This is a difficult question to find the answer to. If a site designer tries some "tricky" maneuvers to fool your browser into displaying something in a unique way, and this crashes your system or freezes your browser, that Web site is probably more trouble than it's worth. Conventional HTML 3.0+ specifications are supported by almost all of the new browsers and should not create a problem on your local machine.

11. Is multimedia appropriately incorporated?
There is a current trend to add background audio or streaming audio/video to Web pages. A good Web page design allows users to choose whether they would like to hear

or see the multimedia. With all the disparate methods and speeds of access to the Internet, this is truly the best way to accommodate everyone.

12. Can the site be accessed reliably at any time of day?
Users of the Internet sometimes fail to realize that, due to the distributed nature of the Internet, the site they are accessing might be sitting on a desktop computer in someone's home. When there is more than one user at a time trying to access that computer, the serving of information may slow down to a crawl. If you are going to use a Web site to provide information for students or to make a presentation, try accessing it at different times of the day. It may be slow during the peak Internet usage times (1pm - 5pm EST), but it still should be usable.

Navigation

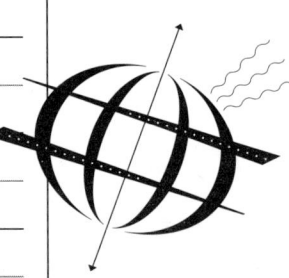

13. If an image map is present, are there also text alternatives?
An image map is a graphic that has pre-programmed hypertext "hotspots" that allow the user to jump to another site or part of the site. An image map is usually a fairly large graphic image, so there should also be text alternatives for the user who doesn't want to wait for the image map to load or for those who can't view graphic images.

14. Are there links back to the home page from the supporting page?
Hypertext allows the user to skip from one place to another on a site without moving in a straight line. Although a strictly menu-based, hierarchical Web site doesn't take advantage of this flexibility, care should be taken to make sure that the navigation buttons back to the top page in the site (called the home page) are present on each page. This helps the user who doesn't know how he or she got there, but just wants to go back to the top of the site, or the user who jumps into the middle of the site from the outside and wants to access the home page.

15. Are name references and anchors used wisely?
A name reference/anchor combination allows a user to jump to a different part of the same Web page. These are very often confusing for the user. If they are present, there should always be a link to the top of the page at whatever point is accessed. A much better design is to place the information on separate Web pages and provide hypertext links to the pages.

16. Do external and internal links work?
Broken links to graphics, as well as external and internal links that produce the "404 Not found" error are all indicative of a Web site that has not been taken care of. It may be out-of-date, abandoned, or ephemeral, and it shouldn't be consulted as a viable source for content information.

17. Is the overall site "user-friendly"?
It is not imperative that a site be easy to use, but it certainly helps the user access the information in a more efficient manner. If the site contains a personal touch, such as a favorite quote or small picture of the author, the user will be more likely to stay and search around the site.

18. Is a search tool available for the site's content?
Some sites include a keyword search to information contained on their own pages. If

this is present, give it a try and see how successful it is. With a well-indexed database, a keyword search can provide a valuable addition to any Web page.

19. Is the resource organized logically for the intended audience/purpose?
The organization of a Web site should be based on the purpose of the site. If the site contains instructions on how to do something (often called a how-to), it should be hierarchical. If there are many avenues of exploration, it should be designed as a branching site. In no case should the design be random. Younger users and beginning Web users need a more clearly defined navigational scheme with fewer choices. Older students may be given more leeway to choose alternative pathways and links. Laura Lemay, in her book *Teach Yourself Web Publishing with HTML 3.2 in a Week*, gives a good description of the types of organization that Web pages might take.[2]

Authorship and Authority

20. Is the page signed with a name and an e-mail address?
Web page authors of any merit should sign their pages with their names and e-mail (or snail mail) contact information. Some larger Web sites may provide an address for only the Webmaster, but any content page should be signed with a specific individual's name.

21. Is information about the author given?
Even if the page is signed, to be sure of the author's ability and knowledge of the topic, it is important that further information be given. The author's résumé, related job history, research interests, and work or school affiliation should be included.

22. Is the author affiliated with a recognized institution?
This criterion may or may not be important in determining the value of a content-rich site. It is assumed that a subject expert would be affiliated with a reputable academic institution. However, some of the most content-rich homepages are created by individuals who are very knowledgeable about a particular topic. One prime example of this would be the *Castles on the Web* site (http://fox.nstn.ca/~tmonk/castle/castle.html).

23. Does the author's affiliation appear to bias the information?
If the page is meant to be an opinion page, and this is stated up front, there is no problem with utilizing the information. However, if the author's affiliation seems to bias the information and it is not obvious that the page may be opinion, rather than fact, the user needs to make sure that the information is verifiable in a second source, and should search for a page that counters this information.

Content

24. Is the purpose/mission of the site stated?
It is very important that the Web page designer provide a brief descriptive paragraph at the beginning of the page that describes the purpose of the site. This helps the user decide immediately if the site will be useful for his or her purpose. This mission statement should also mention the intended audience. A design note: search engines all index the first bit of text that appears on a Web page. So, remember, if you are designing a page, choose these first descriptive words carefully so they are indexed in a usable manner by the search engines.

25. Is the date of last update included?
If timeliness of information is important to the user, this date is a very important element to consider. For information that is not necessarily timely in nature, this date of last update may also indicate the last time that the links were checked and proved valid.

26. Has the site been revised recently?
There are many seemingly useful Web pages on the Net that, when they were produced, were timely and comprehensive in scope. If a site purports to be a list of exemplary Internet links and has not been revised recently, do not take the list of sources as the "best" list of links. Do some searching on your own to come up with newer sites dealing with your topic.

27. Is the information on the site factual in nature?
28. Does the information appear to be opinion rather than fact?
These two questions lead the user to different criteria to evaluate Web sites with different purposes. Jan Alexander and Marsha Tate, from the library at Widener University in Chester, Pennsylvania, recently published an article which provides differing criteria for evaluation of an advocacy page, a business/marketing page, an informational page, a news page, and a personal Web page. It is important that the user determine the purpose of a page before evaluating it. In their article, Alexander and Tate also provide links to sites which demonstrate the various types of Web pages that they describe.[3]

29. Does the site contain original information?
30. Is a bibliography included of the sources/sites consulted?
31. Does the information appear to be accurate? Is it verifiable in a traditional print source?
Any time an author presents original information, the researcher should be able to determine whether the author is familiar with theories or facts in his or her subject area. The author can help the researcher by providing a bibliography of other items consulted. If the author provides a bibliography, it will be easier for the user to verify or disprove the facts presented on the Web page. If the author is refuting an accepted piece of information, the user will still be able to read about the opposing viewpoint and draw his or her own conclusions if a well-balanced bibliography is included.

32. Does the site fulfill the stated purpose?
If a good mission statement is provided at the beginning of a Web site, the user should be able to determine, after examining the site, whether the stated purpose was actually carried out. If the Web site does not live up to the expectations set forth in the purpose, perhaps the user should choose a second site on the topic.

33a. Does the site contain primary-source material?
33b. If the site reports research, are research methodologies and results given?
33c. If the site contains writings, are entire documents included?
If the site provides information about a research project, all details of the research methodologies, sources cited, sources consulted, and data-gathering techniques should be included. If appropriate, enough information should be given for replication of an experiment to verify results.

If the site deals with a published document, the entire document should be present. Little snippets out of context are not usually helpful when examining information.

34. Does the site include links to relevant outside sites?
If the Webmaster is knowledgeable and a recognized expert in his or her subject field, he or she is probably very aware of other sites on the Web that are related to his or her own. If you find a useful, verifiable, authoritative page, the links to other sites are probably also as good. However, don't hesitate to apply all of the criteria in this checklist to any site that you find.

35. Does the site include a form or method of offering comments about the site?
In addition to including an e-mail address, a good Web page has an area for the user to provide to the author a narrative and/or checklist feedback about the site. A good Web page is always improving, and the best ideas often come from the users.

36. Does the content seem to add to the existing body of knowledge about the topic?
Replication of information found in a print source adds to the clutter on the Internet. Some information is best gotten from a traditional print reference book. A content-rich Web page should provide some new information about a topic. This information may be presented in a way that is unique (i.e., via audio, video, or photograph), and/or include new information about the subject.

The technical and design aspects of a Web site, the navigability of the site, the authority of the author, and the content of the site are all interrelated—and should be evaluated as such. All of these criteria need to be considered when evaluating a Web page (or pages) for usefulness. After evaluating a multitude of sites using these criteria, you will find that the evaluation process will become very easy and quick for you. You may also come up with additional subject-specific criteria for evaluation that you will include on your own Web page rating instrument!

References Related to Web Site Rating Form

1 Serim, Ferdi, & Koch, Melissa. (1996). *NetLearning : Why Teachers Use the Internet.* Sebastopol, CA: O'Reilly.

2 Lemay, Laura. (1996). *Teach Yourself Web Publishing With HTML 3.2 in a Week.* Indianapolis, IN: Howard W. Sams.

3 Alexander, Janet E., & Tate, Marsha E. (1996). *Teaching Critical Evaluation Skills for World Wide Web Resources* [Online]. Available: http://www.science.widener.edu/~withers/webeval.htm [1997, May 20].

Critical Evaluation of a Web Site: Elementary School Level

1. How are you hooked to the Internet?
___ Computer and modem
___ Direct connection at school
2. If you are using a modem, what is the speed? *2400   9600   14.4   28.8*
3. Which Web browser are you using? _____
4. What is the URL of the Web page you are looking at?
http:// _____

How does it look?

Does the page take a long time to load? *YES / NO*

Are there big pictures on the page? *YES / NO*

Is the spelling correct on the page? *YES / NO*

Are the author's name and e-mail address on the page? *YES / NO*

Is there a picture on the page that you can use to choose links? (Image map) *YES / NO*

Is there information in columns on the page? (Table) *YES / NO*

If you go to another page, is there a way to get back to the first page? *YES / NO*

Is there a date that tells you when the page was made? *YES / NO*

Do the photographs look real? *YES / NO / NO PHOTOGRAPHS*

Do the sounds sound real? *YES / NO / NO SOUNDS*

What did you learn?

Does the title of the page tell you what it is about? *YES / NO*

Is there an introduction on the page that tells you what is included? *YES / NO*

Are the facts on the page what you were looking for? *YES / NO*

Would you have gotten more information from the encyclopedia? *YES / NO*

Would the information have been better in the encyclopedia? *YES / NO*

Does the author of the page say some things you disagree with? *YES / NO*

Does the author of the page include information that you know is wrong? *YES / NO*

Do the pictures and photographs on the page help you learn? *YES / NO / NO PICTURES*

Summary

Looking at all of the questions and answers above, write a paragraph telling why this Web site is helpful (or not helpful) for your project.

_____

_____

_____

© 1996 Kathleen Schrock (kschrock@capecod.net) http://www.capecod.net/schrockguide/

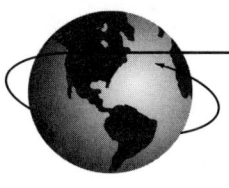

Critical Evaluation of a Web Site: Middle School Level

1. What type of connection do you have to the Internet?
 ___ Dial-in access; modem speed (choose 1) *2400   9600   14.4   28.8*
 ___ Direct connection; (choose 1) *56K   T1   T3   other:* _____

2. Which Web browser are you using?_____

3. What is the URL of the Web page you are evaluating?
 http://_____

Part One: Looking at and using the page

Does the page take a long time to load? *YES / NO*
Are the pictures on the page helpful? *YES / NO / NOT APPLICABLE*
Is each section of the page labeled with a heading? *YES / NO*
Did the author sign his/her real name? *YES / NO*
Did the author give you his/her e-mail address? *YES / NO*
Is there a date on the page that tells you when it was last updated? *YES / NO*
Is there an image map (big picture with links) on the page? *YES / NO*
Is there a table (columns of text) on the page? (You may have to check the source code to tell.) *YES / NO*
 • If so, is the table readable with your browser? *YES / NO*
If you go to another page on the site, can you get back to the main page? *YES / NO*
Are there photographs on the page? *YES / NO*
 • If so, can you be sure that the photographs have not been changed by the author? *YES / NO*
 • If you're not sure, should you accept the photos as true? *YES / NO*

Summary of Part One

Using the data you have collected above, write a paragraph explaining why you would or would not recommend this site to a friend for use with a project.

_____
_____
_____
_____
_____
_____

Part Two: What's on the page and who put it there?

Does the title of the page tell you what it is about? *YES / NO*

Is there a paragraph on the page explaining what it is about? *YES / NO*

Is the information on the page useful for your project? *YES / NO*

  • If it is not, what can you do next? _____

Would you have gotten more information from an encyclopedia? *YES / NO*

Is the information on the page current? *YES / NO*

Does up-to-date information make a difference for your project? *YES / NO*

Does the page lead you to some other good information (links)? *YES / NO*

Does the author of the page present some information you disagree with? *YES / NO*

Does the author of the page present some information that you think is wrong? *YES / NO*

Does some information contradict information you found elsewhere? *YES / NO*

Does the author tell you about himself/herself? *YES / NO*

Do you feel that the author is knowledgeable about the topic? *YES / NO*

Are you positive the information is true? *YES / NO*

What can you do to prove the information is true?

_____

_____

_____

Summary of Part Two

    Looking at the data you have collected in part two, compose a note to the author of the Web site explaining how you are going to use the Web site in your project and what your opinion is of the page's content.

_____

_____

_____

_____

_____

© 1996 Kathleen Schrock (kschrock@capecod.net) http://www.capecod.net/schrockguide/

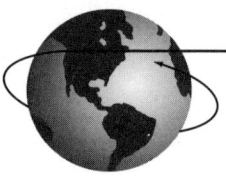

Critical Evaluation of a Web Site: Secondary School Level

Are you using dial-in access? *YES / NO*
- If so, what speed is your modem? *2400   9600   14.4   28.8*

Are you using a direct connection? *YES / NO*
- If so, what type? *56K   T1   T3   Other :*

Which Web browser are you using?
_____

URL of Web page you are evaluating :
http:// _____

Technical and Visual Aspects of the Web Page

Does the page take a long time to load? *YES / NO*
Do the pictures add to the page? *YES / NO / NOT APPLICABLE*
Is the spelling correct on the page? *YES / NO*
Are there headings and subheadings on the page? *YES / NO*
- If so, are they helpful? *YES / NO*

Is the page signed by the author? *YES / NO*
Is the author's e-mail address included? *YES / NO*
Is there a date of last update? *YES / NO*
- If so, is the date current? *YES / NO*

Is the format standard and readable with your browser? *YES / NO*
Is there an image map on the page? *YES / NO*
Is there a table on the page? (You may have to look at the source code to tell.) *YES / NO*
- If so, is the table readable with your browser? *YES / NO*

If you have graphics turned off, is there a text alternative to the images? *YES / NO*
On supporting pages, is there a link back to the home page? *YES / NO*
Are the links clearly visible and explanatory? *YES / NO*
Are there pictures or sounds included?
- If so, can you be sure that the pictures or sounds have not been edited? *YES / NO*
- If you are not sure, should you accept the information as valid for your purpose? *YES / NO*

Content

Is the title of the page indicative of the content? *YES / NO*
Is the purpose of the page indicated on the home page? *YES / NO*
When was the document created? _____
Is the information useful for your purpose? *YES / NO*

Would it have been easier to get the information somewhere else? *YES / NO*
Would information somewhere else have been different? *YES / NO*
  • If so, why? _____
Did the information lead you to other sources that were useful? *YES / NO*
Is a bibliography of print sources included? *YES / NO*
Is the information current? *YES / NO*
Does up-to-date information matter for your purpose? *YES / NO*
Does the information appear biased? *YES / NO*
Does the information contradict something you found somewhere else? *YES / NO*
Do most of the pictures supplement the content of the page? *YES / NO / NOT APPLICABLE*

Authority

Who created the page? _____
What organization is the person affiliated with? _____
Has the site been reviewed by an online reviewing agency? *YES / NO*
Does the domain of the page influence your evaluation of the site? *YES / NO*
Are you positive that the information is true? *YES / NO*
What can you do to prove that it is true? _____
_____
_____

Are you satisfied that the information is useful for your purpose? *YES / NO*
  • If not, what can you do next?
_____
_____
_____

Can you get a printed version of the information? *YES / NO*

Narrative Evaluation

Looking at all of the data you have collected above while evaluating the site, explain why this site is (or is not) valid for your purpose. Include the aspects of technical content, authenticity, authority, bias, and subject content.

_____
_____
_____

© 1996 Kathleen Schrock (kschrock@capecod.net) http://www.capecod.net/schrockguide/

Lesson Plan Instruction:

The following material is provided to help you instruct students, teachers, staff, parents, and anyone else learning this valuable resource.

Lesson: How to Look at a Web Site

Objective: Students will become familiar with the aspects of a quality Web page.

Materials: Overhead projector, overhead transparencies, a copy of the evaluation tool for each student, computer hooked to the Internet with large screen projection device.

Procedure: 1. The teacher will introduce the topic by presenting the transparencies (pages 22-29).
2. The teacher will model an evaluation of an actual Web page using the student evaluation tool and the large screen projection device hooked to the computer.
3. The students, in small groups or individually, will evaluate the usefulness of a Web site for their project.

Evaluation: Discussion of the usefulness of Web sites for particular projects and/or topics.

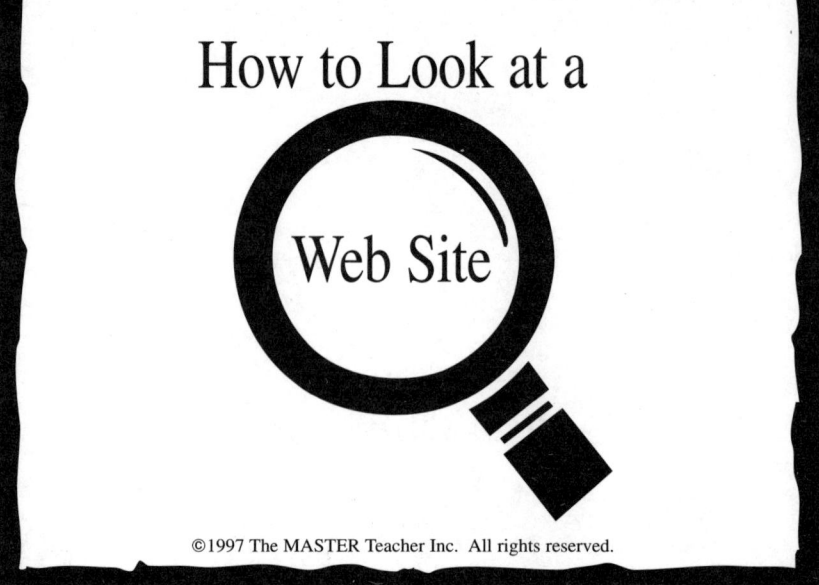

Students should realize that there are five main areas of Web page evaluation:
- Technical and design aspects (How does the page look?)
- Navigation (Is it easy to use?)
- Authorship and authority (Is information about the author included?)
- Content (Is the information correct?)
- Other added value (What else does this site include?)

All of these aspects should be considered together when evaluating the usefulness of a Web page for a particular purpose.

What should you be asking yourself?

- *How does the page look?*
- *Is the page easy to use?*
- *Is information about the author included?*
- *Is the information correct?*
- *What else does this site include?*

©1997 The MASTER Teacher Inc. All rights reserved.

Sometimes, a page takes a long time to load because of "decorative" images. With the current bandwidth restrictions and increased Internet traffic, it is important that students realize that images which add to the information on a Web page are useful, and sometimes necessary, but that extraneous pictures (ones that serve no purpose) are not needed.

It is also important that the page be readable on any machine. For older machines with fewer numbers of display colors, it is best if the page uses simple, contrasting type and background colors.

How does the page look?

- *Do the pictures on the page add to the information on the page?*
- *Do the colors on the page allow it to be read easily?*

©1997 The MASTER Teacher Inc. All rights reserved.

The amount of information that is viewable on a 14" computer monitor browser window is minimal. Because of this, it is important that navigational "cues" such as headings and subheadings of different sizes and colors be used to guide the user through the page.

Due to the hypertext nature of the Web, it is easy to get lost when browsing around a Web site. There should, at the least, be a button back to the main page of the Web site on each page within the site. The use of frames and an ever-present menu may also be used to make navigation more efficient.

The use of an image map, a picture that includes "hot spots" which are actually hypertext links, sometimes adds to the usefulness of the navigation of the page.

Is the page easy to use?

- *Are there headings and sub-headings on the page to help you?*
- *Is it easy to move from page to page within the site?*
- *Is there an image map (a clickable picture) on the page that makes it easier to use?*

©1997 The MASTER Teacher Inc. All rights reserved.

Information in most reliable print reference sources goes through a strict editing process, with an editor verifying the author's experience and credentials.

On the Web, unless a Web site author supplies this information about himself/herself, there is no way to verify that any of the content of the page is correct.

If an author's name, e-mail address, and affiliation are given, the user can always send a note requesting further clarification of ideas or a list of sources used to create the site.

Some pages stay up on the Web long after the author stops updating them, so it is important that a date of last update be current.

Is information about the author included?

- *Did the author sign his/her real name?*
- *Did the author give an e-mail address?*
- *Is there a page with information about the author?*
- *Is the date of the last update of the page included?*

©1997 The MASTER Teacher Inc. All rights reserved.

Because anyone can publish on the Web, it is imperative that students realize that information on the Web should also be corroborated by consulting a reputable print source when possible.

If the information seems to represent only one point of view of a controversial subject (e.g., the death penalty), then it would be helpful for the student to find sites dealing with the opposite point of view and compare and contrast the two.

If up-to-date, breaking news is important to the project, students should realize that there are a several news sites from which to obtain this type of information.

Is the information correct?

- *Can you verify the information found on the Web site in a recognized, authoritative print source?*
- *Does the information provide only one point of view? Can you find other points of view on the Web?*
- *Is up-to-date information important for your project? If so, is this page current?*

©1997 The MASTER Teacher Inc. All rights reserved.

A great Web site is put together by someone who is very familiar with his/her topic and has investigated other sites to compile the page. It is helpful if a Web site provides links to the sites used to create the page or a bibliography of print sources used or sites that offer additional information about the topic.

What else does this site include?

- *Does this site lead you to some other good links on the same topic?*
- *Does this site provide information that you couldn't find anywhere else?*
- *Does this site provide better information than a print source in your school library media center?*

©1997 The MASTER Teacher Inc. All rights reserved.

As more and more original content gets mounted on the Web, sites will appear that contain information that can't be found anywhere else, either digitally or in print. Students should realize that this is a unique and valuable feature of the Web.

Also, as more and more content gets added to the Web, there will be times when the information on the Web may be better (more up-to-date, more explanatory, more comprehensive) than what is available in print in the library media center. It should be pointed out that this will often happen with new discoveries or late-breaking news stories.

Elements of a good Web site:

- *It is easy to use and navigate.*
- *It provides enough information about the author that you can assess whether the author is knowledgeable about the topic.*
- *The information can be verified elsewhere.*
- *The site includes links to other useful sites.*

©1997 The MASTER Teacher Inc. All rights reserved.

Review the aspects of a good Web site with the students to reinforce the lesson.

Center for Teaching
The Westminster Schools

**CARLYLE FRASER LIBRARY
THE WESTMINSTER SCHOOLS**

Instructional Transparencies:

The following pages provide originals for transparencies to be used in teaching students how to evaluate Web sites.

©1997 The MASTER Teacher Inc. All rights reserved.

What should you be asking yourself?

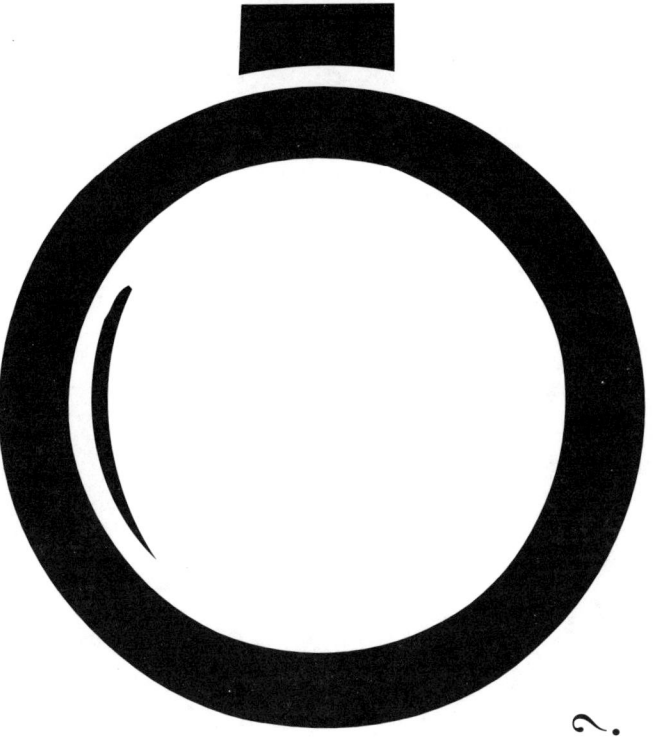

- *How does the page look?*
- *Is the page easy to use?*
- *Is information about the author included?*
- *Is the information correct?*
- *What else does this site include?*

©1997 The MASTER Teacher Inc. All rights reserved.

How does the page look?

- *Do the pictures on the page add to the information on the page?*
- *Do the colors on the page allow it to be read easily?*

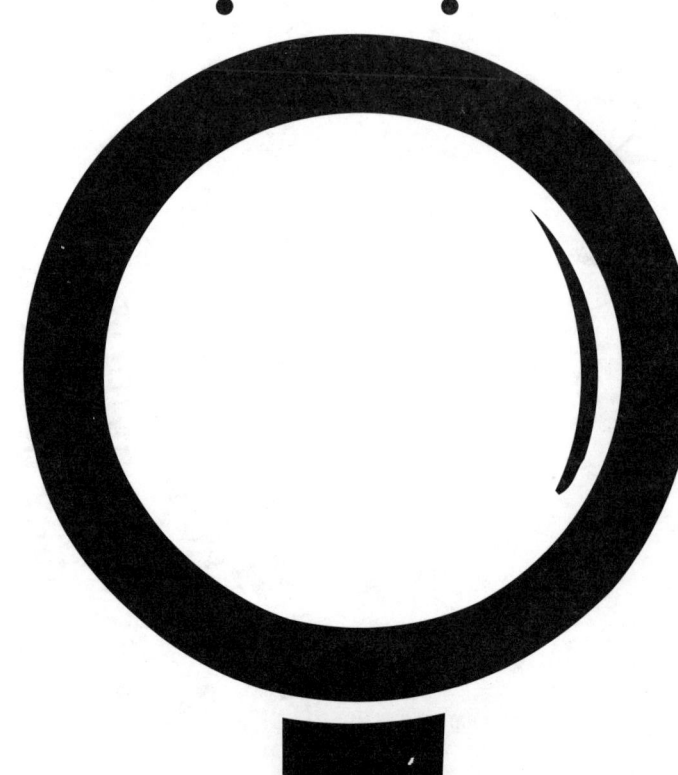

Is the page easy to use?

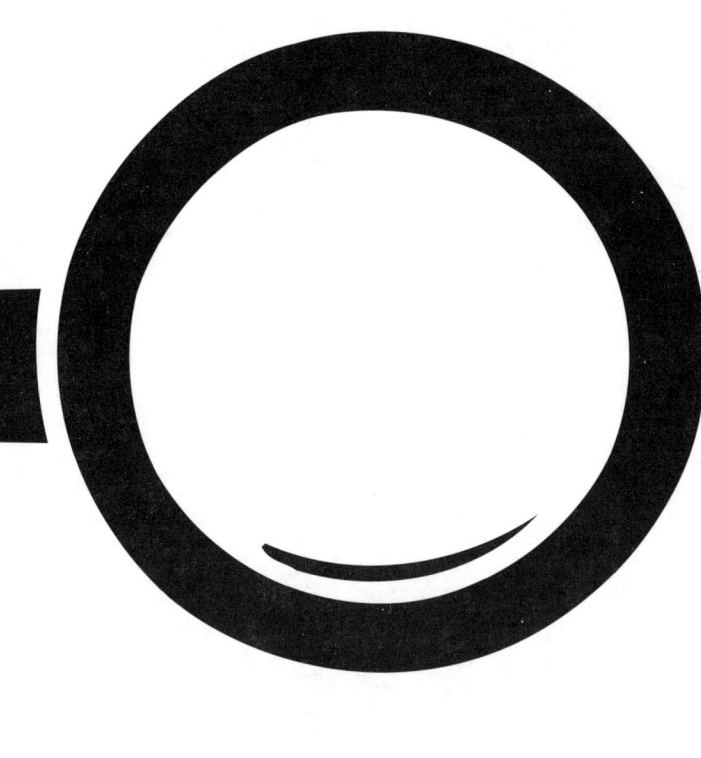

- *Are there headings and sub-headings on the page to help you?*
- *Is it easy to move from page to page within the site?*
- *Is there an image map (a clickable picture) on the page that makes it easier to use?*

©1997 The MASTER Teacher Inc. All rights reserved.

Is information about the author included?

- Did the author sign his/her real name?
- Did the author give an e-mail address?
- Is there a page with information about the author?
- Is the date of the last update of the page included?

©1997 The MASTER Teacher Inc. All rights reserved.

Is the information correct?

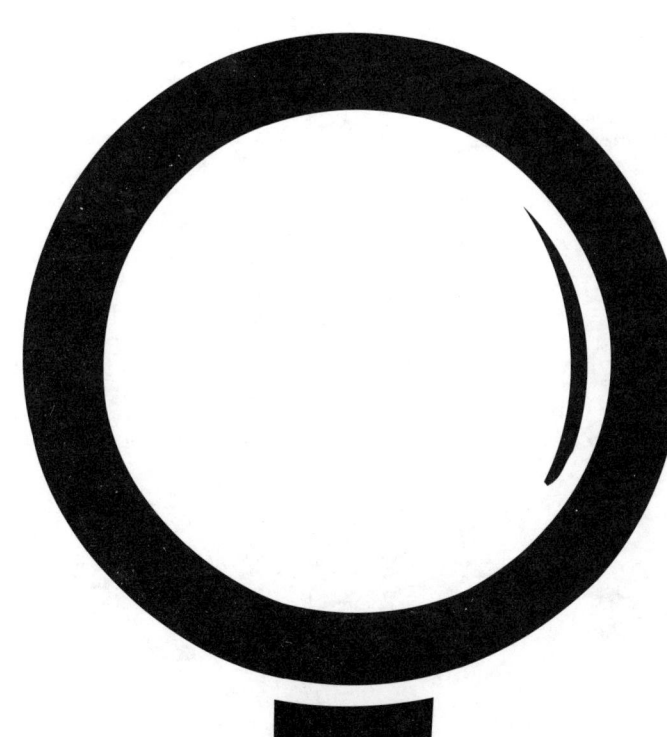

- Can you verify the information found on the Web site in a recognized, authoritative print source?
- Does the information provide only one point of view? Can you find other points of view on the Web?
- Is up-to-date information important for your project? If so, is this page current?

©1997 The MASTER Teacher Inc. All rights reserved.

What else does this site include?

- *Does this site lead you to some other good links on the same topic?*
- *Does this site provide information that you couldn't find anywhere else?*
- *Does this site provide better information than a print source in your school library media center?*

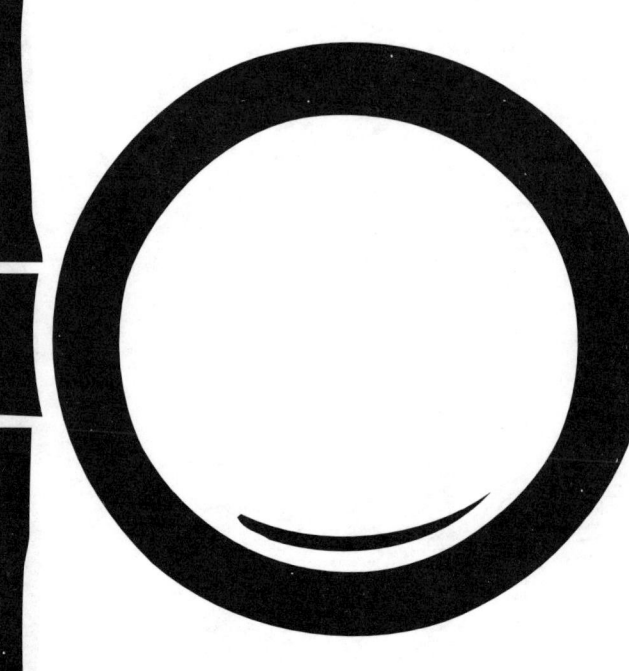

©1997 The MASTER Teacher Inc. All rights reserved.

Elements of a good Web site:

- *It is easy to use and navigate.*
- *It provides enough information about the author that you can assess whether the author is knowledgeable about the topic.*
- *The information can be verified elsewhere.*
- *The site includes links to other useful sites.*

©1997 The MASTER Teacher Inc. All rights reserved.

Glossary

browser The piece of software that interprets the HTML and displays the Web page on your local machine. Four popular browsers are Netscape, Microsoft Internet Explorer, Mosaic, and Lynx.

frame A series of HTML conventions that provide an alternative to traditional navigation by allowing one part of the original Web page to remain present even while you are visiting another.

home page The top page of a Web site; analogous to the front cover of a magazine.

HTML (Hypertext Markup Language) The standardized language that World Wide Web pages are written in to allow for cross-platform use of the Web; also provides the ability to create pages that are linked to other pages.

HTTP (Hypertext Transfer Protocol) The set of rules governing how Web pages are sent and received over the Internet.

hypertext Words that are underlined and shown in color on the Web page. Hypertext terms are linked to other text, and clicking on them enables the user to go right to additional information about the terms. On the Web, these topics are called hypertext links.

image map A graphic that has pre-programmed hypertext "hotspots" that allow the user to jump to another site or a different part of that site.

Internet The global network of millions of computers which are hooked together and communicate with each other.

name reference/anchor An HTML convention that marks a specific point in an HTML document and allows a user to jump from one document to another as well as to a different part of the same Web page.

server A computer that processes Internet inquiries and serves, or sends, the information to the requester.

table An HTML convention that allows information to be put into columns on a Web page.

URL (Uniform Resource Locator) The unique address assigned to each Web site: it may include numbers or the name of the computer where it is housed.

Web page One segment in a Web site.

Web site A collection of related Web pages that are linked together and exist at a particular server.

Webmaster The person who creates a Web site and is in charge of its upkeep.

World Wide Web The part of the Internet that allows hypertext linking of information as well as the incorporation of graphics.

References

Alexander, Janet E., & Tate, Marsha E. (1996). *Teaching Critical Evaluation Skills for World Wide Web Resources* [Online]. Available: http://www.science.widener.edu/~withers/webeval.htm [1997, May 20].

Caywood, Carolyn. (1995). *Library Selection Criteria for WWW Resources* [Online]. Available: http://www.infi.net/~carolyn/criteria.html [1997, May 20].

Elementary School Student's Internet Gateway. (1995). *Evaluating Information: Some Questions to Help You Judge Online Information* [Online]. Available: http://volvo.gslis.utexas.edu:80/~clig/evalinfo.html [1997, May 20].

Engle, Michael. (1996). *Evaluating Web Sites: Criteria and Tools* [Online]. Available: http://www.library.cornell.edu/okuref/research/webeval.html [1997, May 22].

Farrar, Barbara D. (1996). Information Literacy : Retooling Evaluation Skills in the Electronic Information Environment. *J. Educational Technology Systems.* 24(2), pp. 127-133.

Grassian, Esther. (1997). *Thinking Critically About World Wide Web Resources* [Online]. Available: http://www.library.ucla.edu/libraries/college/instruct/critical.htm [1997, May 22].

Janicke, Lisa. (1994). *Resource Selection and Information Evaluation* [Online]. Available: http://alexia.lis.uiuc.edu/~janicke/Evaluate.html [1997, May 20].

Kirk, Elizabeth. (1996). *Evaluating Information Found on the Internet* [Online]. Available: http://milton.mse.jhu.edu:8001/research/education/net.html [1997, May 20].

Ormondroyd, Joan et al. (1996). *How to Critically Analyze Information Sources* [Online]. Available: http://www.library.cornell.edu/okuref/research/skill26.htm [1997, May 20].

Scholz, Ann. (1996). *Evaluating World Wide Web Information* [Online]. Available: http://thorplus.lib.purdue.edu/research/classes/gs175/3gs175/evaluation.html [1997, May 20].

Schrock, Kathleen. (1996). *Evaluation of World Wide Web Resources* [Online]. Available: http://www.capecod.net/schrockguide/eval.htm [1997, May 20].

Smith, Alastair. (1997). *Criteria for Evaluation of Internet Information Resources* [Online]. Available: http://www.vuw.ac.nz/~agsmith/evaln/index.htm [1997, May 20].